Holy Helpmates: Successful Male Female Partnerships Through the Ages

My Secret is Mine, Volume 2

Kristen West McGuire

Published by Secretum Meum Mihi Press, 2024.

HOLY HELPMATES

First edition, January 1, 2024

Copyright © 2024 Kristen West McGuire.

ISBN: 978-0-979-53763-9

Cover art used by permission:

© **Return from Egypt**, by Br. Claude Lane, OSB, Mount Angel Abbey.

Unless otherwise noted, all scripture citations are from the 1899 Douay-Rheims Bible, public domain.

Table of Contents

To Daniel, my helpmate.

And we know that all things work together for good to them that love God, to them who are the called according to his purpose.

Romans 8:28

and

Thank you to Sandra Miesel, whose mentorship and encyclopedic knowledge of medieval history made this series far more interesting and accurate!

Chapter One: What does it mean to be a helpmate?

Is the term "Catholic feminist" an oxymoron? When Edith Stein immersed herself in the thought of St. Thomas Aquinas, she became one. The coherent integration of mind, soul and body for both men and women is a collaborative effort.

Stein struggled in her relationships with men. Her father died when she was two. Her brothers were much older and overshadowed by her mother. Her potential boyfriends during her university years were intimidated by her intensity and intelligence. Her dissertation director, Edmund Husserl, was a father figure to her. Later, his lack of support for her career goals devastated her.

After her conversion, she found more balance in her friendships with men. Her steady prayer life tempered her professional disappointments. And she read St. Thomas Aquinas.

Aquinas said some awkward things about women, based on the limited biology of his day. Somehow, Edith Stein was able to look past the warts and see the beauty of the whole. For Aquinas, form and function pointed to essence, the underlying meaning of life. Thus, the human body has meaning beyond the "accidental" facts of gender difference.

Thus, the creativity of men is oriented toward action, protecting and sustaining life. The physical need for exercise that men experience, and their ability to focus on the task at hand allows them to dominate the created order. Men build castles.

Conversely, women are receptive and nurturing. The feminine ability to conceive and nurse a child implies a gender goal exclusive to women: to bring forth new life, physically, spiritually and emotionally. Women build relationships.

Together, men and women reflect the image of God. But original sin has introduced a rebellion in that union. Edith Stein pointed to two types of rebellions, the opposition of man to God's dominion, and the opposition of the will against the intellect. She notes, "In man, this results in brutish dominance and enslavement to work while the human nature atrophies, while in woman it is seen in servile dependence on men and in sensuality that is not true spirituality, but just a capitulation to the senses."

In other words, men and women need each other. The fullness of human perfection is found in obedience to God and in mastering our passions. Because the receptivity of a woman led to the advent of the Messiah, in the new covenant, women have a unique role to play. Receptivity is prior to creativity.

The Kingdom is not yet fulfilled. Women experience an imbalance of power in daily life, both at home and at work. Even though 60% of American women work outside the home, women fill only a tiny fraction of seats on corporate boards of directors. There are few women leaders serving in the hierarchy of the Catholic Church. And women still perform the vast majority of homemaking, nursing and caregiving chores.

Is this patriarchal oppression? Or does the power of women just manifest itself in a different way? How can men and women work together successfully? The next ten issues of Secretum Meum Mihi will explore these questions.

Each chapter highlights a historical pair who worked together for the sake of the Kingdom. The essay and historical sketch will highlight their enduring contributions to the Church. The bible study and book review will add deeper meaning to their stories, and highlight the particular virtues they perfected in this life. And we will pray to become the change we wish to see in the world.

As it happens, Pope Benedict indicated that he intended to install some women in higher Vatican offices and did so before he died. Further, Pope Francis appointed three women to the Dicastery of Bishops, the Vatican office which selects candidates for new bishops.

No matter who sits in the hot seat, men and women were created to work together. We cannot take the kingdom by force, nor can we force others to love as Jesus taught us. Love is discovered by practicing it. To serve is to reign.

Bible Study: Genesis 2:15-25

Return to the Garden

^{15}*And the Lord God took man, and put him into the paradise for pleasure, to dress it, and keep it.* ^{16}*And he commanded him, saying: Of every tree of paradise thou shalt eat:* ^{17}*But of the tree of knowledge of good and evil, thou shalt not eat. for in what day soever thou shalt eat of it, thou shalt die the death.* ^{18}*And the Lord God said: It is not good for man to be alone: let us make him a help like unto himself.* ^{19}*And the Lord God having formed out of the ground all the beasts of the earth, and all the fowls of the air, brought them to Adam to see what he would call them: for whatsoever Adam called any living creature the same is its name.*

^{20}*And Adam called all the beasts by their names, and all the fowls of the air,*

and all the cattle of the field: but for Adam there was not found a helper like himself.

^{21}*Then the Lord God cast a deep sleep upon Adam: and when he was fast asleep, he took one of his ribs, and filled up flesh for it.* ^{22}*And the Lord God built the rib which he took from Adam into a woman: and brought her to Adam.* ^{23}*And Adam said: This now is bone of my bones, and flesh of my flesh; she shall be called woman, because she was taken out of man.* ^{24}*Wherefore a man shall leave father and mother, and shall cleave to his wife: and they shall be two in one flesh.* ^{25}*And they were both naked: to wit, Adam and his wife: and were not ashamed.*

(Douay Rheims Bible, 1899)

Context: There are two accounts of the creation of man in the book of Genesis. The first, in Genesis 1:1 - 2:4, emphasizes the essential unity of man and woman before the Lord, and their twofold mandate to exercise dominion over the natural world, and to be fruitful and multiply.

The second account here emphasizes the incompleteness of man without woman. This account of the bliss of Eden is untainted by power issues, which arose after the fall. The essential harmony of their relationship is depicted by their lack of shame.

Translation: Scholars believe that the first creation account is a compilation done by priests of the Temple, possibly even prior to the first Babylonian exile (about 500 B.C.) The second is more human centered, and yet retains evidence that it began as a story told and retold by Mesopotamians over the centuries. (Its similarities with the Babylonian creation epic, *Enuma Elish* are striking.)

Vocabulary:

Eden: derived from a Sumerian word meaning "fertile plain," Eden connotes a similar Hebrew word meaning "delight"; the Greek word in the Septuagint means, "paradise."

"helper like himself:" eser k'negdo: (helpmate) Eser is a derivative of help, which shares a root that means strength (oz). The root of k'negdo means opposite or "in front of." It's usually translated "corresponding to him." Clearly, it does not imply subservience, but mutual strength.

"one flesh": modern translations usually say "one body"; classical Hebrew has no specific word for "body." The sacred writer stresses the fact that conjugal union is willed by God.

Meditation: Adam recognized Eve. He was probably getting tired of naming creatures. It's lonely at the top of the food chain! Although he apparently slept through the rib extraction, he knew enough to call her his own.

God could not create His own image in only one gender. His goodness overflows. So, a man needs a woman to truly embody the goodness of God. Is it too much of a stretch to posit that woman was created to ensure that man enjoyed AND labored?

A baby's first learned response is the smile, when Junior recognizes the embrace of the loving caregiver and crinkles his little eyes in response. The baby "recognizes" the love, and responds.

The first account of Genesis emphasizes one fact that the second account forgets to mention. God was very pleased, and even enjoyed his creations. Together.

In all relationships, men and women find that they bring differing and complementary strengths to the table. Obedient to their calling, women have a unique gift for enjoying the fruits of the earth and celebrating God's gifts. Likewise, men recognize in women the key to a proper ordering of his work before the Lord.

Discussion Questions:

1. Are there differences between men and women in what evokes a smile? Why is that? Which would you call the result of original sin? Which are "primeval?"

2. There seems to be an inner compass that helps us recognize a friend. It's easy to love those who are like us. The intimacy of Adam and Eve in the garden was related to that recognition of shared humanity – and the absence of sin. How can we create little pockets of Eden in today's world?

3. The prevalence of lust in modern society has changed interactions between men and women in many ways. How do we see ourselves as changed by encounters with lust? How does the experience of authentic love heal those effects of sin?

Chapter Two: Saints Peter and Mary Magdalene

Priest, Prophet and King: On Receiving Our Vocations

In a series on successful male-female partnerships, St. Peter and St. Mary Magdalen are an unlikely example. The Bible records only one interaction between them, when Magdalen tells Peter that the Lord has risen. The gospel accounts differ, but it seems Peter ran to see the empty tomb for himself, and did not believe her. They certainly were not close friends.

The contrast between them could not be more stark. While Peter is mentioned hundreds of times in scripture, Magdalen's name pops up exactly thirteen times. There are medieval traditions and unofficial accounts (rejected by the Church) about both Peter and Mary Magdalen, with the latter drawing more attention today. The gap between history and myth is very large.

All the gospels agree on two facts. Jesus chose Peter to be the leader of his twelve man crew. And Jesus chose to appear to Mary Magdalene first after His resurrection. I'm not inclined to believe these were arbitrary choices. Jesus gave each a job to do, and they did, in fact, do their work well enough that everyone remembered it.

Don't we often get lost in the details ourselves? It's hard to know which tasks are most needful. During the Lord's Passion, Peter variously refuses to have his feet washed at the Lord's Supper, falls asleep on sentinel duty, nearly slices an ear off a guard, and then runs away at the crucial moment.

Magdalen has a better showing under pressure. Alongside the Blessed Mother, Magdalen, Salome, and the other women did not abandon Jesus for one minute, witnessing both his death and his burial. Devastated with grief, Magdalen goes to the tomb with spices to anoint the body, numbly clinging to Jewish rituals for burial. Just as her grief was total, so then was her joy!

If only she could convince the disciples of the truth! Despite a history that included the Transfiguration and Jesus walking on water, we have the future Pope essentially rejecting the prophetic witness of the Lord's anointed messenger, Mary Magdalen. Mercifully, Jesus arrives on the scene to corroborate Mary's story.

Jesus orchestrates a massive fish haul on the beach one morning. Peter's thick head leads Jesus to ask him repeatedly, "Do you love me?" This is not an auspicious beginning for Christendom. The fact is, neither Peter nor Mary Magdalen asked for their respective roles in salvation history. Jesus himself chose them.

Because Mary Magdalen spent the majority of Jesus' ministry following the disciples, and providing for them out of her means (Luke 8:1-3), I am inclined to believe she went back to that role after Pentecost.

And Peter overcame his doubts and impulsivity to capably lead the Church with the help of the Holy Spirit. His death by crucifixion followed in the path of Jesus. His preaching introduced thousands of people to Jesus. In the end, he did his job for the King.

Mary Magdalen's prophetic witness came PRIOR to the apostles preaching the good news. Her prophetic witness might have been initially rejected by the apostles, but that did not invalidate her faith, nor render her actions useless. Once the King intervened, the disciples had to see women in a new way. Tell me that wasn't necessary to the King's plan!

Am I saying that the early Church was free from sexism and blatantly false assumptions about the capabilities of women? No. But Christianity through the ages has created more opportunities for women than any other religion. Jesus had great confidence in the women who served him in first century Palestine, and he has great confidence in you and I today.

No, the Church wasn't perfect then, and it isn't perfect now. This isn't heaven. But, we can perform our part of his mission on earth. Jesus is the one who gives both men and women parts to play in his earthly ministry, be it as a priest, a prophet or a king. My guess is that Peter and the apostles never forgot who first encountered the Lord. Nor should you!

Historical Sketch: The Location of the Upper Room

The Upper Room served as a hiding place for the apostles in the days immediately following the crucifixion of Jesus. Understandably, they thought they might be next in line on Pontius Pilate's hit list. Then, it was a place to ponder and praise the resurrection of Jesus. Small wonder Christians over the centuries have zealously sought out the actual room!

Like many sites in the Holy Land, the building is sacred to Jews and Muslims as well. King David's Tomb rests in the basement. Damage during the war for Israeli independence allowed archaeologist Jacob Pinkerfeld to excavate the site while repairing it, and he found five different levels of flooring. The Upper Room has endured a variety of foundations. Pinkerfeld first found a 12th-century Crusader floor, just beneath the marble slabs. A mosaic floor with geometric designs dating to the Byzantine period rested about eighteen inches below that. A mere four inches lower, the remains of the original Roman floor were revealed, constructed at the end of the first century.

The original building appears to have been a Judeo-Christian synagogue, abandoned when Titus destroyed Jerusalem in 70 A.D. Almost the entire city was left in ruins. When Emperor Hadrian visited some years later, he reported that only the neighborhood on Mount Zion survived, including a small "Church of the Apostles," which was supposedly built atop the original Upper Room.

Byzantine Emperor Theodosius the Great erected a larger church, Hagia Zion, in the late fourth century, built on top of the older ruins. Bishop John II of Jerusalem elevated it to Basilica status in 415. The Persian army destroyed most of the land's churches, including Holy Zion, in the early seventh century. After the Persian withdrawal, the Christians rebuilt it, but in the early 11th century an apocalyptic caliph from Egypt flattened it again.

When the Crusaders rebuilt it, they combined the Church of the Apostles and the Church of the Pillars (built to honor the final resting place of Mary the Blessed Virgin), naming the new church St. Mary of Mount Zion. The building housing the Upper Room and King David's Tomb is separate from Dormition Abbey, but their underlying foundations link up with the ancient ones described above.

Tourists visiting the Upper Room today find a large room with three naves, and gothic style columns worthy of the Crusaders who constructed them. A Muslim mihrab points the direction of Mecca for daily prayer, reminding the visitor of the many occupants of the building over the centuries. Several yeshiva schools (for the study of the Torah) dot the neighborhood, in honor of the Davidic lineage housed below.

Each successive construction to honor the birthplace of Christian joy had a unique character. It is somehow fitting that, 2000 years later, the Upper Room and its basement burial chamber draws thousands of tourists each year. King David symbolized the messianic hope of the Jews, and the Upper Room became for Christians a witness to the answer to those prayers.

Discussion Questions:

1. In the Upper Room, the disciples first were told that Jesus had risen, by St. Mary Magdalene. Only later would the Holy Spirit fall on the apostles in this same room. Have you ever experienced a life changing moment that caused you to carry forward the memory of a place?

2. The disciples didn't believe Mary Magdalene until they encountered the Risen Lord themselves. This is very common – and a good reminder to us that conversion truly is inspired by Jesus himself. Have you ever questioned the veracity of someone's conversion? Or, experienced others questioning your faith? How did you respond?

3. Jesus revealed his resurrection first to a woman...in the tomb. Do you believe women have a special gift for prophecy? Can you give any examples from your personal experiences?

Chapter Three: Saints Paula and Jerome

Laying Down Your Life for a Friend

The young widow Paula and her daughter Julia Eustochium and a company of ascetic virgins abruptly left Rome in 385. Their friend Jerome had quit the city a month previous, and discreetly awaited them in Cyprus. The gossips in Rome were correct; the group was headed to Palestine, together. They eventually settled in Bethlehem, and established two monasteries, including a scriptorium for Jerome's intellectual work, and schools for both the monks and the nuns.

The tongues wagged for a reason. Jerome's tactlessness alienated many matrons in the city after his arrival in 381 to serve as a scribe for Pope Damasus. He quickly made a name for himself, and the pope weighted his service highly as an ascetic and a scripture expert. His extensive travels and experience as a hermit in the wilds near Antioch further added to his exotic cachet. He was of an age to be noticed, at the top of his game.

Paula was descended from prominent Roman families, and had lost her husband in 379 at the young age of 32. She begged Jerome to teach the scriptures at her home, where like-minded virgins gathered to support one another in a sacrificial lifestyle.

Patient and detail-oriented, Paula mastered Hebrew so well that she could chant the Psalms in Hebrew without a Latin accent. But her accomplishments merely egged on their detractors: an old man tutoring young women, wasting his time "studying the scriptures."

Jerome appreciated Paula's zeal and spiritual insights on the scriptures, while she revered his accomplishments as a scholar. They were indeed soul-mates, though not in the way that lascivious Roman minds thought.

Jerome's true passion was scholarship, and notwithstanding his devotion to ascetical practices, his sanctity developed from his studies. During his travels throughout the empire, Jerome listened and studied the languages and dialects, and made friends with native speakers. When he finally settled in Bethlehem, he was prepared to begin his life's achievement, the translation of the original Hebrew and Greek Bible into Latin to produce the Vulgate Bible.

Although Paula handled most of the logistical details of building the monasteries, Jerome did teach the monks and nuns to read the Scriptures, and even taught young boys the classical Latin texts, work that he found most satisfying. Paula didn't do all of his copywork; he received stipends for copyists from benefactors.

Paula's provided a safe house for Jerome. She lived the ideals he so zealously promoted throughout his career. In return, he provided an outlet for her intellect and wealth. In keeping with their spiritual friendship, he curbed some of her more excessive penances. It is doubtful that he would have finished his translation of the Vulgate without her stabilizing influence.

Jerome stopped writing for several months after her death in 404 at the age of 56. He was simply speechless. Eventually, with Eustochium taking the reins of the monastic leadership, he finished the last few books of his Vulgate translation. When Eustochium also died in 418, Jerome was again completely undone. His grief drips from the words of his letters, until his own death two years later.

Did Jerome merely use Paula and Eustochium to further his own intellectual accomplishments? Or did he honor their sacrifices by serving the Church with a Vulgate translation and treatises on monasticism that presaged the work of Benedict? We won't know about the fairness factor this side of the veil. However, we do have the record of a doctor of the Church taunting his male detractors with the fact that Paula and Eustochium were better Hebrew scholars than most men of his acquaintance.

Who's zoomin' who? Is it oppression to provide a place for souls to rest, or to spend a lifetime helping another gifted man to achieve brilliant successes? Edith Stein says, "...whoever makes her will captive to God in this way can be certain of a special guidance in grace." (Essays on Woman, p. 124) Heroic sanctity attracted many followers to their desert abode, proof of such guidance.

Although the Church celebrates only Jerome's contribution to biblical scholarship, I fully expect the Bibles in heaven to bear the following inscription: to the saints Paula and Eustochium, who birthed the Vulgate.

Bible Study: I Corinthians 12:4-13

Many Gifts and Talents, But Only One Lord to Serve

Now there are varieties of gifts, but the same Spirit;

and there are varieties of service, but the same Lord;

and there are varieties of working, but it is the same God who inspires them all in every one.

To each is given the manifestation of the Spirit for the common good.

To one is given through the Spirit the utterance of wisdom, and

to another the utterance of knowledge according to the same Spirit,

to another faith by the same Spirit,

to another gifts of healing by the one Spirit,

to another the working of miracles,

to another prophecy,

to another the ability to distinguish between spirits,

to another various kinds of tongues,

to another the interpretation of tongues.

All these are inspired by one and the same Spirit, who apportions to each one individually as he wills.

For just as the body is one and has many members, and all the members of the body, though many, are one body, so it is with Christ.

For by one Spirit we were all baptized into one body—Jews or Greeks, slaves or free—and all were made to drink of one Spirit.

Context: St. Paul was in Ephesus on his third missionary journey when he received word that the Corinthian church had "issues." Its membership was quite diverse, so much so that many members were literate enough to seek their own answers to some of the questions they posed to Paul. This passage on the unity of the "Body of Christ" comes after a key section on the centrality of the Eucharist in the life of the faithful Christian.

Translation: St. Paul was a typical Jewish Pharisee of his day. He read the Old Testament in the Greek Septuagint, but his written Greek betrayed his Hebraic origins. St. Jerome later complained of his lack of elegance as a Greek stylist. His theological insights, however, were first-rate.

Vocabulary:

gifts: *Greek charisma* - a spiritual endowment, given by God

service: *Greek diakonia* attendance as a servant, aid, service, ministry

working: *Greek energema* – an effect, result of working, or operations that have effects, derived from energeo to be active, effectual, to just do it!

utterance: *Greek logos* the word as in spoken word (refers to Word in John 1)

wisdom: *Greek sophia* wisdom won through skill; insight; understanding

knowledge: *Greek gnosis*, spiritual/experiential aspect of knowledge, connotes a systematic treatment or a proof

Meditation: There are indeed talented Christians out there, and the gifts strewn at the altar are amazingly diverse. It's easy to see how disputes might arise about the relative worth of the gifts, and even the givers. Humility is a necessary gift from every giver.

In many parishes, about ten percent of the people do ninety percent of the work. But is it fair to say that the rest are merely freeloading off the efforts of the few? Sometimes. But what if the "work" simply isn't suited to the gifts that the other members bring to the altar? What if we are missing out on many gifts, simply because the frenetic pace of modern life is keeping us ignorant of the gifts that others are too busy or too overwhelmed to share?

If God wants the job done, He'll send the workers to the vineyard. But we must be sure that the hours of the vineyard are conducive to work, and that the overseers are sensitive to the needs of the workers. And, sometimes, we might have to redefine "necessary work." Will we spend less time in purgatory if the annual chicken dinner gets bumped off the calendar one year? I'm not sure, but it's worth asking the question.

Discussion Questions

1. Have you ever felt that your gifts were not appreciated in the parish? Has Jesus helped you find somewhere else to share your gifts?

2. The unity we seek is offered to us in the love of Christ Jesus. Thank someone in your parish this week for his/her gifts, especially if you suspect that the person often isn't noticed. Then, pray for unity in your parish, whether it already exists or not

3. Because men have most of the authority in parishes, some strange power dynamics can happen with female staff. For example, even though the church secretary is not ordained, sometimes she has a powerful role as a gatekeeper for the pastor. What are the positive and negative effects of such relationships? How can women effectively exercise leadership in the parish?

Chapter Four: Saints Scholastica and Benedict

No Grumbling Allowed!

Fish swim, birds fly...and children grumble.

Whether it's comparative dessert or chores, most children are uniquely qualified to comment on the relative inequities of family and society. Mothers shake their heads and sigh, trying to judge fairly and yet keep chaos at bay. The needs of the monastery (and domestic church) dictate a certain level of personal sacrifice, no matter how many monks and nuns reside within.

I use this tendency to my advantage with my two youngest, ages two and three. When one notes that the other has my attention, he'll do anything to re-direct it back to himself. Thus, they unwittingly play into my hands, ending up on an even schedule of meals, baths, stories and naps.

I'm sure Benedict and Scholastica's mother was less cunning, and more gentle. The Rule of St. Benedict contains much that would be considered feminine wisdom in most households, including reminders to the abbot and those in authority not to lead in such a way that causes grumbling. Benedict's wisdom was as hard-won as any mother's could be. One set of monks tried to poison him!

Consider the following excerpts from the Rule of St. Benedict:

"Similarly, [the abbot] should so regulate and arrange all matters that souls may be saved and the brothers may go about their activities without justifiable grumbling." (Ch. 41)

and

"Let him strive to be loved rather than feared...therefore drawing on examples of discretion, the mother of virtues, he must so arrange everything so that the strong have something to yearn for, and the weak have nothing to run from." (Ch. 64)

In fact, Benedict mentions the "evil of grumbling" frequently within his short rule, and he exhorts the brothers to put up with, "a little strictness," in order to "safeguard love." Most men of my acquaintance would scoff at such concerns. Strictness is a means to test and harden the body as it assaults the elements and duties of life, or so my Marine husband tells me. But that kind of masculine strictness can also bind love in chains.

The little we know of St. Scholastica indicates the generosity and piety of her family. She was consecrated to the Lord from a young age. (If I were to give the Lord any of my progeny, the boys would be my first choices. My girls are helpful to me!)

Benedict was sent to school in Rome, where the parade of immorality shocked him into a hermitage. Once he was established in a monastery at Monte Cassino, Scholastica followed him to live in a little hermitage nearby, perhaps with a few other women.

The one consolation Benedict allowed himself as abbot was his yearly conference with Scholastica. Sisters are wise and loyal counselors.

As we go through life, our siblings know us perhaps better than anyone, and they also are privy to our deepest longings. When Scholastica insisted that Benedict stay to discuss the joys of heaven with her, he nearly rebuffed the gift of God...by grumbling about the weather she asked from the Lord!

We are so used to grumbling to our siblings, that it is almost natural. And yet, is it natural? Or just a habit? Is it possible that both Benedict and Scholastica were surprised to be at odds again, even with the maturity of their faith? Of course!

I'm sure he completely repented when her death made the gift clear in hindsight, and reminded him in no uncertain terms that the love of the family trumps even man-made Rules. Sometimes, when our grumbling partners remind us of important truths, we remember them well.

May we be open to the love of God in our families, and especially, in our siblings!

Bible Study: Numbers 12: 1-15

Miriam and Aaron Caught in Sibling Rivalry

Miriam and Aaron spoke against Moses because of the Cushite woman whom he had married, for he had married a Cushite woman; and they said, "Has the Lord indeed only spoken through Moses? Has he not spoken through us also?" And the Lord heard it.

Now, the man Moses was very meek, more than all men that were on the face of the earth. And suddenly the Lord said to Moses, and to Aaron and Miriam, "Come out, you three, to the tent of meeting."

And the three of them came out. And the Lord came down in a pillar of cloud, and stood at the door of the tent, and called Aaron and Miriam; and they both came forward.

And he said, "Hear my words: If there is a prophet among you, I the Lord make myself known to him in a vision, I speak with him in a dream. Not so with my servant Moses; he is entrusted with all my house. With him I speak mouth to mouth, clearly, and not in dark speech; and he beholds the form of the Lord. Why then were you not afraid to speak against my servant, Moses?"

And the anger of the Lord was kindled against them, and he departed; and when the cloud removed from over the tent, behold, Miriam was leprous, as white as snow. And Aaron turned toward Miriam, and behold, she was leprous.

And Aaron said to Moses, "Oh, my lord, do not punish us because we have done foolishly and have sinned. Let her not be as one dead, of whom the flesh is half consumed when he comes out of his mother's womb."

And Moses cried to the Lord, "Heal her, O God, I beseech Thee." But the Lord said to Moses, "If her father had but spit in her face, should she not be shamed seven days? Let her be shut outside the camp seven days, and after that, she may be brought in again." So Miriam was shut up outside the camp seven days; and the people did not set out on the march till Miriam was brought in again.

Context: The book of Numbers takes up the story of the people of Israel after the Exodus from Egypt, but before they take possession of the Promised land. This story is confirmation that there was dissension and unhappiness among the rank and file as they struggled to survive in the desert.

Translation: Scholars believe that this book was written in the fifth century B.C., by priests concerned with explaining the many liturgical norms and sacrifices codified after the Jews returned from their exile by the Persians. It is one of the five parts of the of Jewish Torah, the books of the Law.

Vocabulary:

the man (Moses) was very meek: The plural in Hebrew for this word "man" is *anawim*, which has idealistic overtones of piety, while *anayv* ("meek") connotes affliction, poverty and sanctity in suffering.

mouth to mouth: This expression is found nowhere else in the Hebrew scriptures. This speaks to the unique character of Moses' relationship with God.

she may be brought in again: All lepers were considered unclean, and this is the basis of Miriam's banishment, but it is clear from the context that God heals her, otherwise she would not have been allowed back into the camp.

Brothers and sisters know all our dirt, don't they? And envy seems to take up residence at every family dinner table. Despite clear evidence that Moses was God's anointed, his imposed-upon siblings had to speak up, and air the dirty laundry, too. (Find me the political family without issues, please!)

Alas, God has plans for all of us much bigger than our petty complaints about one another. Not only does God clearly rebuke Miriam and Aaron, but places Moses in the position of delivering Miriam from her fate. After a short exile, she is welcomed back. And the camp moves on.

Discussion Questions:

1. Have you ever been tempted to criticize a family member publicly? Did you? How did your relationship change as a result?

2. Although we aren't the wandering tribes of Israel, we often need to "move on" after unpleasant family episodes. Especially at Thanksgiving, what can you do to be a peacemaker in your own "camp?"

3. Often, our perceptions of family drama change as we age. How have your perceptions changed? What helps families find healing and reconciliation?

Chapter Five: St. Radegund and Venantius Fortunatus

In Praise of Shared Beauty

I wonder when Radegund first conceived the idea of becoming a nun. Perhaps during her early childhood in her uncle's home, when she learned he killed her father?

Or, around the age of reason, after her family was decimated by the Franks, when she was carried off by Clothar to become his wife in training? Did she know then?

Perhaps she knew when Clothar's other wives bore children at the time of her marriage?

Or, more likely, ten years later, when Clothar murdered her only surviving brother?

She finally left him then, and sought to live as a religious in a villa that was part of her dower. Eventually, Archbishop Germanus of Paris had to intervene to keep Clothar from reclaiming his prized "possession."

When he finally died in 561, Radegund was able to establish a monastery in Poitiers with ample funds from Clothar's desire for absolution prior to departing this life. She dedicated the rest of her life to providing a haven for women like herself who had been abused by the violence of the era.

Venantius Fortunatus arrived on the scene in Poitiers and began a friendship with Radegund and her spiritual sister Agnes that lasted two decades. Their shared love of poetry and beauty was healing to both. Venantius abandoned his troubadour lifestyle, and settled there, dedicated to showering his beloved with poetry that survived the murderous age in which they lived.

It may seem odd to highlight a pair like Fortunatus and Radegund at Christmas. Even the hymns that Fortunatus is famous for honor the Holy Cross, and seem more appropriate for Lent.

But there are many who are not surrounded by a large and loving Christian family, and whose friends provide needed succor and strength all through the year. The beauty of friendship is a gift worthy of the Magi, who hoped to be counted among the friends of the newborn King.

Especially for women who may have endured violent and humiliating treatment at the hands of the Clothars of the world, I propose a toast this Christmas to all those men who bring forth beauty in the lives of women, and honor their accomplishments so that history will not forget about them.

To the Lady Radegunde with a Bunch of Flowers

O Queen, that art so high

Purple and gold thou passest by,

With these poor flowers thy lover worships thee.

Though all thy wealth thou hast flung far from thee,

Wilt thou not hold

The violet's purple and the crocus' gold?

Take this poor offering,

For it thy thoughts shall bring

To that blest light that is to dawn for thee,

Fields bright as these, and richer fragrances.

And when thou comest there,

Hear, O my Saint, my prayer,

And may thy kind hand draw me after thee.

Yet, thou thine eyes

Already look on flowers of paradise,

These thine own flowers

Would have thee out of doors.

Yea, thou the flowers of paradise are sweet,

These fain would lie Where thou wert passing by.

(reprinted from Helen Waddell's out of print but lovely translation of Venantius Fortunatus found in *Medieval Latin Lyrics*.)

Bible Study: Psalm 131

Like a Child Quieted at the Breast

A Song of Ascents

Of David.

O LORD, my heart is not lifted up,

my eyes are not raised too high; I do not occupy myself with things too great and too marvelous for me.

But I have calmed and quieted my soul, like a child quieted at its mother's breast; like a child that is quieted is my soul.

O Israel, hope in the LORD from this time forth and forevermore.

Context: The book of Psalms is actually a collection of several smaller "songbooks" of ancient Israel. Psalm 131 is part of a collection known as the "Songs of Ascents" which were likely sung by pilgrims headed to Jerusalem to the Temple. The Temple site itself was located on Mount Moriah, and the city was surrounded by the Judean hills on three sides.

Translation: Although it is traditional to assume that King David composed the Psalms, scholars cannot confirm that conclusively. This particular collection of songs were probably dated later, perhaps even after the Babylonian exile and rebuilding of the Temple. The last line appears to be a "liturgical" addition.

Vocabulary:

lifted up: Other translations of this word are haughty, and with the next line, even arrogant. The humility of the pilgrim is childlike, looking for direction.

quieted: also translated frequently as "weaned", the original Hebrew *gamal* connotes a ripening or benefit. The psalmist plays off the quiet receptivity of the child secure on its mother's lap with the anxiety of making a pilgrimmage.

Anyone who has traveled with children in tow can appreciate the beauty of this Psalm during the holiday rush to reunite across the miles. Humbling ourselves *en route* is even an imitation of our Lady, who arrived in Bethlehem in peasant style.

Even if we expect no pilgrimmage this Christmas, the Christ Child will make His appearance to all souls. If we receive Him, the infant Jesus resides with us and we carry Him wherever we go, including to the Temple. Can you trust your own ability to provide for the life of Christ within? Trust in the Lord! He shall indeed provide!

Discussion Questions:

1. Every adult has had the childhood experience of condescension. Sometimes, we also experience that humiliation as adults. How do you react to being treated as a child? Why?

2. The quiet soul of the child on his mother's lap is a beautiful image of Christmas. Find your favorite from among this year's cards, and imagine yourself on Mary's lap alongside baby Jesus. What might happen if you joined their idyllic repose regularly?

3. Children find delight in the newness of a journey. How can we access delight instead of drudgery when shepherding young ones across great distances?

Chapter Six: St. Christina of Markyate and Geoffrey of St. Albans

A Powerful Female Spiritual Mentor

Our 12th century heroine, Christina of Markyate, dreamt in Technicolor, with visions beginning in girlhood. The story of her life has an unmistakably medieval flamboyance. She had a notable devotion to the Blessed Virgin Mary, but it wasn't a quiet piety. Her imitation of Mary skewed toward the dramatic, outflanking and destroying enemies by the sheer magnitude of her talents, emboldened by her faith.

Christina was seen as a prized possession by her Anglo-Saxon family, who hoped to marry her off advantageously with a Norman aristocrat. Beautiful, passionate, intelligent and obstinate, she defended her vow of virginity in theological and legal terms, in addition to traditional prayers and asceticism. Christina's character was a unique blend of Marian piety and manly prudence.

Christina's story might never have been told without her best friend and patron, Geoffrey de Gorren. Ironically, he was the conniving and worldly French abbot of St. Albans. After the two shared a mystical vision of heaven, Geoffrey was convinced that Christina's intercession was crucial to the eternal salvation of the monks entrusted to his care.

Geoffrey's monks at St. Albans were not so sure. Rumors swirled about Christina. At the time Geoffrey met her, she was a recluse, in her own hermitage bequeathed to her by her spiritual mentor, Roger. Her unorthodox "novitiate" was directed by this elderly ascetic, who took her in when she fled from her conniving family. He tested her resolve with severe penance. By day, she hid in a small storage room attached to Roger's chapel, curled up in order to fit, and locked in, let out only once a day to urinate, and subject to extreme temperatures.

After four years of near constant prayer, Christina was ready to be set free, legally and spiritually. Through it all, Christina credited the comforting visions of Blessed Virgin for her endurance. However, it is just as true that her male patrons enabled her cherished independence.

Christina attracted other Anglo-Saxon women, founding a Benedictine enclosure near St. Albans Abbey. Abbot Geoffrey diverted resources to the nuns, provoking grumbling among his monks. When Geoffrey commissioned the St. Albans Psalter for Christina and her nuns, the expensive gift may have shocked the monks, who withdrew the abbey's funding of Christina's group immediately after his death in 1147.

A treasure of medieval literature, the St. Albans Psalter is prized as a window into the linguistic effects of the Norman Conquest. It includes miniatures of the life of Christ in which there are many women depicted, and the Alexis Quire, a story of chaste St. Alexis in both Latin and French, thought to be a language tutorial for Christina. The psalter includes several depictions of the adulation of Geoffrey and some of his frères for saintly Christina.

Although temporally dependent on the monks, Christina was her own spiritual maverick. Did Christina need Geoffrey? Many women find that a male patron can provide the "street cred" for a woman to exercise leadership. She had the gravitas to make the monks quiver, one way or another. I suppose it could be called oppression to be so dependent upon a man for legitimacy.

Every era provides its own challenges for leaders. All of Christina's early experiences prepared her to lead others to a strong and pure love of Christ. Her story is a testimony that God will not abandon those who trust in His Mother. Christina of Markyate should be the patroness of women unafraid to trust their leadership skills and experience.

May the powerful intercession of the Blessed Mother inspire you!

Historical Sketch: Converting One Lusty Priest After Another

by Sandra Miesel

Sexual harassment is hardly a modern invention. And like so many of life's problems, there's a saint who suffered it. The saint in question is the colorful but obscure Christina of Markyate (1098-1157) who defended her virginity with courage and resourcefulness. Providence rewarded her patience.

Christina was the daughter of a wealthy Anglo-Saxon couple in Huntingdonshire, England. She'd originally been named Theodora ("Gift of God") because an omen involving a dove had led her mother to anticipate a specially blessed child. With her spiritual adviser's permission, pretty and pious Christina took a private vow of virginity at age 16.

But shortly thereafter, Christina unwittingly caught the eye of the lecherous bishop of Durham, Ralph Flambard. He'd previously kept Christina's aunt as his concubine and had two children by her. When seduction failed, he tried to rape Christina but she escaped by a ruse. She rejected his attempt to sweeten her response with gifts.

Out of malice, Flambard arranged an unwelcome marriage for Christina with a nobleman named Burthred. After a year of heavy family pressure, Christina was forced to sign a betrothal agreement. Escaping the marriage meant escaping consummation. In those days no special wedding ceremony was required, just a promise to marry followed by intercourse established a valid marriage.

Christina's family stopped at nothing to push the advantageous match to conclusion. For more than a year, they confined Christina, dosed her with drink and magic potions, and even encouraged Burthred to rape her. But Christina managed to wiggle away each time. She even won an annulment from her bishop but it was reversed through bribery.

Finally, after a savage beating by her mother, Christina escaped home disguised as a man. The pageboy who helped her deception was killed. Christina hid with a nun for two years and then for another four with a holy hermit. To preserve secrecy at the hermitage, she was shut up in a tiny cupboard during the day, which she spent in prayer.

Burthred eventually released Christina from the betrothal with an apology. The Archbishop of York confirmed her freedom but put her under the protection of a prominent cleric. Unfortunately, the new protector made sexual advances at Christina, too. She subdued her own temptation to respond through prayer and penance. The abashed priest withdrew his attentions.

Now Christina was free to take public religious vows, first as a hermit, then as prioress of a new convent at Markyate. She was a wise superior for her own nuns, rallying them through two disastrous fires. She embroidered vestments for the English Pope Adrian IV and struck up a warm spiritual friendship with Abbot Geoffrey of St. Albans. She turned him from worldliness to piety and kept him safe through her prayers. Here at last was a man whom Christina could cherish with "a wonderful but pure love," holding to him in the face of slander. Geoffrey died in 1147, Christina a decade later.

Discussion Questions:

1. Our culture has its own challenges to chastity for young maidens. Are young women safer today than in the Middle Ages? How can one safeguard against the dangerous sin of lust?

2. Because of the many documented cases of clerical sexual abuse, it is not a shock to read a story about a lecherous cleric today. But it might have seemed shocking 100 or 1000 years ago to your average parishioner. How have the sexual abuse scandals of the Church affected your parish? Your personal faith?

3. How do you turn others from worldliness to piety? What does it mean to put heaven first in our lives today?

Chapter Seven: Saints Francis and Clare

In Defense of Lady Poverty

War changes things. Within Assisi, opposition between "old money" nobles, such as Clare's family, and the "new money" merchants, such as Francis' family, was virulent. When riots erupted in Assisi, Clare's family took refuge in neighboring Perugia. The disparity between rich and poor was easier to see as a refugee. Clare was deeply moved.

When the battle engulfed both towns, aspiring knight Francis was imprisoned for over a year in Perugia, and later battled only illnesses instead of other knights. His dreams of glory dashed, Francis gradually found solace in simplicity and nature.

When marriage plans surfaced for her, Clare contacted Francis for advice. She had likely heard him preach in the plazas in Assisi.

Clare "followed" Francis, leaving her family home on Palm Sunday in 1212. However, her writings reveal her own independent, charismatic vocation. In Francis, she found a spiritual brother, in whom God had entrusted a parallel devotion to "Lady Poverty."

After a few dramatic "rescue" attempts, Clare's family accepted her vocation. Her simplicity and holiness attracted other young women, and even impressed a Bohemian princess so much that she started a similar convent. Their only contact with the world was through Francis and his followers, who pledged support to the poor ladies in a spirit of mutual love and unity. After all, they were brothers and sisters of the poor baby Jesus, who had nowhere to lay his head.

The dominant model for male-female relationships in Western culture is the parasite. Men and women use one another's talents and weaknesses, jockeying for relative power and immediate gains. Because we are all weak, few are immune to this way of thinking about worldly success.

Both Francis and Clare turn power and prestige upside down by asserting the primacy of poverty. In this gospel model, we are receptive before we are active. The goodness within each human heart, and the goods we receive to preserve our lives are actually the gifts of God. The only thing we can actually be said to own is our sins and failings, our discomforts and disillusionments.

Everything else is actually given to us by God— resources, talent, zeal, opportunity and creativity are merely manifestations of God's plan for us in the world. Thus, it is impossible for humans to be parasites, unless they accept a vision for their lives that is less than fully human.

The partnership of Francis and Clare points to this gospel vision of equality in a radical way. Both were rooted in a loving appreciation for our weaknesses, and a joyful trust in God's strength to deliver us. Even in good partnerships, it happens that one sacrifices "more" than the other. The ideal is for each person to give without counting the cost, toward the good of the other. Sacrifices are offered as gifts, and counted as gifts by the other.

Francis and Clare were gifts to one another. They kept each other in check. Francis came back to San Damiano and saw that he was not crazy, that his Poverty ideal could be lived. And at the same time, he kept Clare from living it a little too well.

Clare was serious about being a servant. For example, Clare insisted on changing the mattress ticks for the sisters. Bugs were attracted by the white cloth that they stuffed with straw. It was disgusting work. But when she started filling her own mattress with twigs, Francis intervened and ordered her to stop.

Francis again interceded when Clare over-did the penitential fasting. Although it was voluntary, Francis understood the dangers of ascetical practice. Sometimes, you can fast (or abstain) for reasons that have more to do with ego, or pride in your own strength. Her health actually was already compromised by the rigors of the vocation she lived. For the sake of prudence, Francis reminded Clare that refusing the meager fare provided to the community was to refuse the good gifts of God.

There was a healthy give and take in the life-giving love that they shared. Clare held fast to their ideals, devoted to Lady Poverty and cultivating the community of nuns to follow her example. Francis provided limits and protection from the outside so that these same ideals remained life giving and not a source of death.

Both Francis and Clare turned the battle inward, shaking the human heart free of the things of this world that imprison souls. Their love of poverty wasn't an impossible ascetical ideal, but a prophetic witness to the bounty of God's love for us.

For those of us surrounded by the bounty of material things, it is a welcome reminder this Lent to "go to war" with our attachments and pride. Alongside Francis and Clare, we can learn what it means to be a gift of God to the world.

Bible Study: Luke 9:51-62

The Son of Man Has Nowhere to Lay His Head

And he sent messengers ahead of him, who went and entered a village of the Samaritans, to make ready for him; but the people would not receive him, because his face was set toward Jerusalem.

And when his disciples James and John saw it, they said, "Lord, do you want us to bid fire come down from heaven and consume them?" But he turned and rebuked them.

And they went on to another village.

As they were going along the road, a man said to him, "I will follow you wherever you go."

And Jesus said to him, "Foxes have holes, and birds of the air have nests; but the Son of man has nowhere to lay his head."

To another he said, "Follow me." But he said, "Lord, let me first go and bury my father."

But he said to him, "Leave the dead to bury their own dead; but as for you, go and proclaim the kingdom of God."

Another said, "I will follow you, Lord; but let me first say farewell to those at my home."

Jesus said to him, "No one who puts his hand to the plow and looks back is fit for the kingdom of God."

Context: This excerpt is the turning point in Jesus' life. After Jesus "sets his face toward Jerusalem," every story in Luke's gospel must be read through the lens of His Passion and Resurrection. The rejection of the Samaritans reveals that the Israelites were fighting over the identity of the chosen people of God. Jesus will be rejected in Jerusalem as well. In their zeal for the Messiah's honor, the disciples show the Messianic expectations that fueled the infighting. The Kingdom would be very different than the disciples or the Israelites expected.

Translation: Although the original prophetic literature was recorded in Hebrew, Jews in Luke's day heard the Greek Septuagint read aloud. Luke's word choices allude to the Old Testament prophets Elijah and Elisha, (see I Kings 19:19-21), as well as the apocalyptic prophet, Ezekiel, who was told specifically to "set his face AGAINST Jerusalem," and to prophesy against the land. (Ezekiel 21:7-8) Luke sounds severe, but he is proposing that Jesus came precisely to fulfill these prophecies in a new and radical way, through poverty.

Vocabulary:

for him to be received up: The word *analempsis* is used once in the entire New Testament— right here. Compare this to II Kings 2:1, where Elijah was about to be taken up by the Lord in the whirlwind.

deliberately set his face to: Luke renders this passage in the Greek *sterizo*, with the word *prosopon*, literally "he hardened his face to go," a combination which mimics numerous passages in the book of Ezekiel. The apocalyptic character of Jesus' action is thus heightened. This is not just a journey to Jerusalem, but one that extends all the way to Jesus' resurrection and ascension.

"farewell to those in my home": The Greek *apotassomai* (to say farewell) is used elsewhere to refer also to possessions. Literally, it means saying goodbye to everything contained in one's house.

For Francis and Clare, this passage was foundational. Not only was Jesus poor materially, but his poverty included obedience to the Father oriented toward Jerusalem, toward the cross.

The Blessed Mother is their "Lady Poverty." She gave birth in a stable, and sought refuge in Egypt. Hot showers and fine linen weren't part of her package deal. After Jesus began his earthly ministry, he gave her the time of day exactly once, at Cana. The radical gospel supercedes even family ties. She received the Messiah so that she could give Him to us.

In a world obsessed with control, we sometimes forget that life is a gift of God. We receive a beating heart and the breath of life; we do not control them entirely. As Christians, our lives are joined to the person of Christ, and thus we become the gift of Jesus to the world, a gift for others.

So, when the disciples around you are scheming to control unruly Samaritans, remember that Jesus came to smash our expectations about the Kingdom. Turn yourself to the business at hand and become the gift. If you journey alongside Jesus to Jerusalem, God will provide.

Discussion Questions

1. Sometimes when money troubles find us, we later note how the priority challenge was a good corrective. What priorities are competing for your checkbook? Have you juggled them lately?

2. Mother Teresa said, "Poverty is love before it is obedience." Instead of focusing on renunciation this Lent, what loves in your life are leading you to Jerusalem? Away from Jerusalem?

3. Our awareness of poverty is often episodic. But for many people, it is an unwanted lifestyle imposed by cruel fate. What do we owe to persons whose poverty we see? How can we learn?

Chapter Eight: Saints Teresa of Avila and John of the Cross

Madre Teresa was fifty-two years old when she met twenty-five year old Fray Juan de Yepes, a Carmelite novice at Salamanca. She needed reliable confessors for her nuns in the reformed monasteries.

Given the facts, likely Juan was caught off-guard by Teresa's style. Sunny, personable and determined, Teresa seemed to be his opposite. Inexperienced, artistic and deeply ascetic, Juan yearned to unite his simple joy in creation with the poverty of Christ. Teresa recognized his sanctity, noting in her journal that she could learn more from him than he could learn from her.

They were a study in contrasts. Juan's family had been a part of the "army" of beggars created by a severe food shortage in Castile. A locust scourge in 1542, followed by years of meager harvests and disease decimated the already impoverished families of the region. His father died when he was a toddler. His mother moved three times in five years. Successful begging was the special Yepes family charism. Little Juan often begged for those unable to do so. Thus, he and his elder brother Francisco were known for charity!

Wealth and honor belonged to Teresa's family, but they were not without suffering. Teresa's mother died at thirty-three after bearing nine babies, leaving teen-aged Teresa with a negative attitude toward the physical hardships of marriage. Pretty and vain, Teresa nonetheless fell in with a merry group of boy-crazy cousins, irritating her grieving father.

He sent her to boarding school to break up the group, where she discovered some of the joys of religious life. Her father was shocked when his favorite daughter entered the Convent of the Incarnation in 1536. Teresa fell ill, perhaps from malaria, and spent most of her novitiate recuperating, nearly dying in 1539.

Even after her father died in 1543, she loved the less-than-sacred elements of life at Incarnation. Many of the nuns didn't belong in a convent at all, and carried on with visitors in scandalous ways. Teresa was one of the more virtuous, comparatively speaking. She had a special way of reaching out to souls, and once she dedicated this faculty to the Lord alone, her path to sanctity was steady.

Thus, in 1567, Juan confided a deep secret to Teresa: he was having vocational doubts, inclined to leave Carmel for the Carthusians. Teresa deftly reminded him of the depth of his devotion to Our Lady of Mount Carmel. With the sureness of purpose that marked all of her work, she believed the Lord sent Fray Juan to her. Eventually, he decided to wait while she made the arrangements to form the first monastery of reformed Carmelite friars.

The first monastery at Duruelo was a dilapidated farmhouse, barely better than a pigsty. On his journey as the first friar of the discalced Carmelites, Juan carried a habit tailored by Madre Teresa, and walked barefoot as the friars were "discalced," or shoeless. (Ironically, Teresa prudently forbade the "discalced" friars to walk barefoot in the winter.)

Fray Juan reveled in two months of solitude, setting up the monastery prior to the arrival of three more in November 1568. His joy was palpable.

During Advent, la Madre managed to visit her pet project. She was mildly disturbed by the profusion of crosses and skulls adorning the little "Stable of Bethlehem." While meant to remind holy souls of the last things, the mother's heart in Teresa was stirred. While she approved of their prayerful lifestyle, she "begged them not to be so rigorous in penitential practices." At the same time, their obvious joy in the new foundation was contagious, and she "went away greatly consoled."

The gifts of the Lord for the two friends went both ways. Madre Teresa helped Juan to find his place among the Carmelite friars, renaming him Fray Juan de la Cruz. Years later, Fray Juan would repay her amply by providing spiritual direction to her and the nuns at the Incarnation, when Teresa was prioress from 1572-1575.

Motherhood cuts both ways. It brings with it deep responsibilities, but also sublime self-knowledge and above all, the joy of sharing love. May your motherly relationships be a source of resurrection for you this Easter!

Historical Sketch: John and Teresa, Just Levitating Together

Saint Teresa of Avila became prioress of the monastery of the Incarnation in Avila in October 1571. It was the monastery of her profession, where she spent nearly thirty years of her life. After she began her reform houses in 1562, she never expected to come back. Even if no man is a prophet in his birthplace, Teresa's superiors were confident she would clean up the mess.

The Incarnation included some women seeking to escape the demands of life in the world, in addition to genuine vocations. Teresa knew her higher standard of service out of love would be difficult to impose by mere rules. Well aware of the deep-seated spiritual malaise of the large institution, Teresa sent an adamant request for John of the Cross to sign on as confessor for her 180-odd nuns.

As usual, her request was honored. John arrived in May 1572, and set about hearing confessions, offering talks on spirituality. The "calced" friars still offered confessions, but Teresa counted on the winning ways of her prime padre to pull in the recalcitrant. He did. Writing out little sayings on small slips of paper, and offering keen observations with loving overtones, he was soon their favorite friar.

Teresa found his help invaluable. Although she had already written her autobiography and the *Way of Perfection*, she had begun to write her masterpiece, the *Interior Castle*. Under Padre Juan's experienced guidance in 1572, she experienced the fullness of loving union with God, which she described as the seventh mansion.

On Trinity Sunday, 1573, the two saints were seated on opposite sides of the grille in the speakroom. Their intense conversation on the Trinity, combined with prayerful exhortation, was not interrupted when Teresa's niece, Beatriz de Cepeda y Ocampo, entered the room.

Before her eyes, Teresa was levitating, oblivious to her presence. Through the grille, she could see John of the Cross was also aloft, and even his chair! Such events of ecstasy were not uncommon for Teresa in her later years, who sometimes had to have her nuns hold her down when she began to levitate during public liturgies.

Teresa joked about it later, blaming it all on saintly John, "You can't speak about God with Fray Juan de la Cruz because he gets carried off in ecstasy and carries others off with him."

When they first met, Teresa gave John a Carmel worthy of his unique talents. But ever after, it was John's gift to offer the Carmelite family his deeply "uplifting" outlook on life, including his *Dark Night*.

His 1577 imprisonment by jealous calced friars only led to a greater good. The poetry he composed as a prisoner is acclaimed by secular experts. His internal freedom defied all worldly bonds. No one could hold the holy man down, and he lifted many to the honors of the altar with him.

Discussion Questions:

1. Have you ever had an experience of suffering that led to other people growing in faith? Describe the situation. What did you learn from it?
2. Do you believe in stories of supernatural phenomena like speaking in tongues or levitating? Why or why not? What would change your mind about such things?
3. The saints seem so lofty to us. Instead of giving up on sanctity, perhaps it is easier to listen for the next step. What's your next step? What difficulties are you finding in taking that step? Why?

Chapter Nine: St. Elizabeth Ann Seton and Archbishop John Carroll

The First American Saint and the First American Bishop

When newly widowed Elizabeth Seton returned to New York in 1804, her Protestant friends and relatives tearfully greeted her at the harbor. It was the last public display of support she received from them. Her decision to become a Catholic nearly a year later outraged them; she endured constant persecution and withdrawals of previous promises of aid.

Elizabeth and William Seton sailed to Italy in November 1803, seeking a Mediterranean cure for his tuberculosis. Quarantined in a dank prison cell upon his arrival, he died six weeks later. However, the months Elizabeth spent grieving with their Italian Catholic friends, the Filicchi family, were decisive for the future of American Catholicism.

Even before the revolution, John Carroll's family thrived despite the persecution. Trained and ordained by the Jesuits in Europe, he returned to the colonies after his beloved Society of Jesus was disbanded by papal edict in 1773. The American Jesuits signed agreements with a London bishop to stay and serve their persecuted sheep. Deprived of financial support for their missions, many were inclined to ecclesiastical disobedience.

In 1776, Carroll accompanied his famous cousin, Charles, on his unsuccessful mission to woo the French Quebecois to the patriot cause. Fr. Carroll returned to his mother's farm in Maryland, and politely avoided questions about his future.

After the war ended, a prominent priest, Wharton, apostasized and published his reasons. Because Carroll had served as a university professor before the suppression, the public response fell to him. By most accounts, Carroll's humble but intelligent essay easily debunked Wharton's *apologeia*. Meanwhile, Carroll administered sacraments, and promoted education, notably Georgetown College.

His eloquence and tactful advice in frequent matters of local dispute won him the respect of clerics and laity. The American Catholic flock continued to grow. Itinerant Catholic priests showed up throughout the land, some without any oversight from ecclesiastical authority. A leader was needed, but most priests feared a Protestant backlash if the Vatican appointed a bishop.

Elected by his peers and ratified by Pope Pius VI, Carroll was consecrated a bishop in 1790. When a national synod notable for its collegiality resulted in greater uniformity in Catholic doctrine and practice, he returned his attention to Catholic education. The boys' schools were thriving, but what about the girls? The foreign orders he approached declined his overtures. Carmelites and Poor Clares were cajoled about expanding their mission. No one budged.

Elizabeth Bayley Seton's precarious financial and social situation in New York evolved into the answer to Bishop John Carroll's prayers. As early as 1806, Sulpician Father William Dubourg encouraged Elizabeth to contact the bishop about her desire for convent life. Surprised, she did contact Carroll, who responded affirmatively some six months later. When Cecelia Seton, Elizabeth's sister-in-law, converted, the Seton family became openly hostile to Elizabeth and her children.

There was even a minor riot on Christmas Eve 1807 at St. Peter's Church, related to the public disapproval of the Catholic Setons. It was time to leave New York. Dubourg offered Elizabeth the use of a house in Baltimore for a school.

She arrived in Baltimore in June 1808, and soon attracted students and young postulants to help teach. Amazed at providence, she set about her pedagogical and motherly duties. (Her youngest child was barely school age at the time.) Her holiness, gradually attained under fire in New York, reassured Carroll that she could handle both physical and spiritual maternity.

Things moved quickly. By the spring of 1809, Elizabeth had secured the funding to establish the Sisters of Charity in Emmitsburg, Maryland. Bishop Carroll finally had his foundress! Despite his concern over her children, Carroll consecrated Elizabeth to religious life as the prioress of the new Sisters of Charity on the feast of the Annunciation 1809. She was known as Mother Seton ever after.

Truth is stranger than fiction. Who could have predicted the successful growth of the American Catholic Church, founded by a priest of a suppressed order and a persecuted widow with five children to raise? Both are witnesses to the strength and independence of Catholic Americans and our openness to the promptings of the Holy Spirit, even today.

Catholic women can take heart in Mother Seton's example! All things were possible because she believed. Don't let the obvious obstacles in your life keep you from being open to the wildest possibilities that faithful obedience brings to your doorstep.

Bible Study: Acts 14: 8-18

Paying Homage to Church Leadership

8 Now at Lystra there was a man sitting, who could not use his feet; he was a cripple from birth, who had never walked. 9 He listened to Paul speaking; and Paul, looking intently at him and seeing that he had faith to be made well, 10 said in a loud voice, "Stand upright on your feet." And he sprang up and walked.

11 And when the crowds saw what Paul had done, they lifted up their voices, saying in Lycaonian, "The gods have come down to us in the likeness of men!" 12 Barnabas they called Zeus, and Paul, because he was the chief speaker, they called Hermes.

13 And the priest of Zeus, whose temple was in front of the city, brought oxen and garlands to the gates and wanted to offer sacrifice with the people. 14 But when the apostles Barnabas and Paul heard of it, they tore their garments and rushed out among the multitude, crying, 15 "Men, why are you doing this? We also are men, of like nature with you, and bring you good news, that you should turn from these vain things to a living God who made the heaven and the earth and the sea and all that is in them. 16 In past generations he allowed all the nations to walk in their own ways; 17 yet he did not leave himself without witness, for he did good and gave you from heaven rains and fruitful seasons, satisfying your hearts with food and gladness." 18 With these words they scarcely restrained the people from offering sacrifice to them.

Context: Paul was well-educated for a Jewish man and Roman citizen. While he understood the pagan errors of these Greek onlookers, he couldn't let them offer sacrifices to him, pretending he was Hermes, or Barnabas was Zeus! Tearing their garments was a very evocative sign, reminiscent of the high priest in the Jewish temple, rending his garments in the face of sacrilege. Authorities were nearby checking out these apostles of the Crucified One, who claimed that he was God. Some Jews wanted to distance themselves from the new Jewish-Christians, who, by this time, were incurring their own unwelcome attentions from Rome.

Translation: Classically educated listeners would have recognized in this story the myth of Zeus and Hermes visiting a pious couple near Lystra, from Ovid's *Metamorphoses*. Because the locals are speaking in the Lycaonian dialect, Paul and Barnabas are unaware of the developing problem until the high priest of Zeus shows up in his glad rags, ready to bow down to the "gods!" Paul appeals to their philosophical awareness of good, especially natural goods, to defuse the situation.

Vocabulary:

Zeus: The king of the gods, also known in Roman parlance as Jupiter.

Hermes: understood to be the spokesman for the gods, also known as Mercurius.

To rend their garments: the Greek *diarrhesso* is only found in the New Testament in relationship to the high priest "rending" his garments in pain at sacrilege.

of like nature: The King James version reads, "of like passions with you," because the underlying Greek *homoiopathos* implies a mortal subjectivity, not divine detachment.

Meditation: How do we interact with the princes of the church? In the recent past, the bishops have surely had their comeuppance. Once, Catholics literally bowed and kissed their bishops' rings in deep devotion. Today's bishops prefer a more casual approach to all interactions.

Not unlike the pagans, we seem to make gods of men whom we see doing great miracles. And if the bishops aren't exactly miracle workers, well, we'll keep our oxen and garlands to ourselves, thanks.

Paul understands the dynamic. Just like these Zeus worshippers, we all need to remember that the apostles and their successors are "subject" to passions, just as we are. The power is there, but power shifts, relative to context. It's no basis for eternity.

The bishop's exalted state is precisely derived from eternity! God directs him to proclaim the good news, that Christ died to set us free from our passions, free to love with the deepest and most abiding security. What we can't see, and what the Lyconians did see, was plain in the miracle before their eyes. Miracles do still happen. The challenge is to see them.

Discussion Questions

1. What is the proper way to show respect when one meets a bishop? Is it possible to overdo it? Do we show disrespect for the church if we underdo it?

2. A bishop who leads based on "eternal" issues often endures "bad press." Is it anti-Catholicism? Or just criticism?

3. Our popular pagan deities today are not Zeus and Hermes, but Britney Spears and Paris Hilton. How do you counter their influence in your home? School? Parish?

Chapter Ten: Saints Louis and Zelie Martin

Parents of St. Therese, the Little Flower

More than one nun has confided to me that she was forcefed a spiritual diet of the "Little Way" of St. Therese during her novitiate. It's an acquired taste, at least for some. Although Therese is a doctor of the church and widely invoked today, her wisdom is more readily apparent after life's experiences buffet our complacency.

The Martins weren't exactly your average Catholic family. Both Louis Martin and Zelie Guerin attempted to join religious orders in early adulthood and were rejected. Louis lacked the Latin scholarship necessary for the priesthood, and Zelie's fragile health disqualified her. They met in Alençon, and recognized one another as soulmates.

Louis Martin was a watchmaker by trade, and a happy bachelor. His mother had noted devout Zelie at Mass, a successful lacemaker. Zelie's sister, a Visitandine novice, received a tearful visit from the bride as the wedding approached. Zelie mourned her dream of religious life and was fearful of the physical toll of motherhood.

Louis also was distracted by spiritual yearnings and shared Zelie's misgivings. So, when the Martins married in 1858, they resolved to undertake a chaste lifestyle. After ten months of marriage, their parish priest ordered them to consummate the marriage.

The charm of their firstborn completely changed the couple. Louis reportedly told the priest at the baptism, "This is the first time you have seen me here for a baptism, but it won't be the last!" Mmm-hmmm. They had eight more children in thirteen years, but only five survived to adulthood: Marie, Pauline, Leonie, Celine and Therese.

Louis Martin was a modern helpmate of a husband, long before it was fashionable. Zelie supervised a cadre of more than a dozen lacemakers, in addition to competently running the household. Louis sold his business in 1871 and often traveled back and forth to Paris, visiting buyers and suppliers. Zelie kept up the business pace, even as her health failed after 1873, a testimony to her amazing energy. She worked hard!

Zelie had no time for village gossip and frittering away time in useless frivolities. She did write many letters to her siblings, and from these, we can learn of the zeal with which she mothered her brood. Although her own childhood as a military brat was unhappy and marked with a rigor of religious practice, her children experienced her joy in life and obvious pride in their beauty and intelligence.

There were plenty of worries and tears. They hired wet-nurses and servants to help them handle the domestic load. In at least one case, the wet nurse failed in her duties, and the poor infant starved to death. Reading between the lines, both Leonie and Therese had sensitive ears and Leonie had a severe learning disability with allergies. (See the historical sketch on page eight.) This isn't heaven.

After Zelie died in 1877 from breast cancer, Louis sold the lace business and moved to Lisieux to be closer to family. The voluminous correspondence among the girls testifies to his solicitous care of them after their valiant mother's death. They didn't just esteem heaven because Zelie was there. The family made heaven real in their love for one another.

All five girls entered religious orders. One might worry that the girls were coached to seek the religious life that had eluded their parents. But, "the joy of the Lord was their strength." Louis and Zelie grounded their family in the confidence of God's mercy.

The story of the "Little Way" has spread the Martin family's joy to millions of people! That's a pretty good earthly return on an investment of spiritual yearning.

Bible Study: *Job 1:8-12; 2:4-10; 42:10-17*

Job's Wife Copes While Job Philosophizes

And the LORD said to Satan, "Have you considered my servant Job, that there is none like him on the earth, a blameless and upright man, who fears God and turns away from evil?"

Then Satan answered the LORD, "Does Job fear God for nought?

Hast thou not put a hedge about him and his house and all that he has, on every side? Thou hast blessed the work of his hands, and his possessions have increased in the land.

But put forth thy hand now, and touch all that he has, and he will curse thee to thy face."

And the LORD said to Satan, "Behold, all that he has is in your power; only upon himself do not put forth your hand." So Satan went forth from the presence of the LORD.

(Job's children die and his wealth disappears.)

And the LORD said to Satan, "Behold, he is in your power; only spare his life."

So Satan went forth from the presence of the LORD, and afflicted Job with loathsome sores from the sole of his foot to the crown of his head.

And he took a potsherd with which to scrape himself, and sat among the ashes.

Then his wife said to him, "Do you still hold fast your integrity? Curse God, and die."

But he said to her, "You speak as one of the foolish women would speak. Shall we receive good at the hand of God, and shall we not receive evil?" In all this Job did not sin with his lips.

(Job philosophizes with three onlookers. No details on his wife are recorded.)

And the LORD restored the fortunes of Job, when he had prayed for his friends; and the LORD gave Job twice as much as he had before.

Then came to him all his brothers and sisters and all who had known him before, and ate bread with him in his house; and they showed him sympathy and comforted him for all the evil that the LORD had brought upon him; and each of them gave him a piece of money and a ring of gold.

And the LORD blessed the latter days of Job more than his beginning; and he had fourteen thousand sheep, six thousand camels, a thousand yoke of oxen, and a thousand she-asses.

He had also seven sons and three daughters.

And he called the name of the first Jemi'mah; and the name of the second Kezi'ah; and the name of the third Ker'en-hap'puch.

And in all the land there were no women so fair as Job's daughters; and their father gave them inheritance among their brothers.

And after this Job lived a hundred and forty years, and saw his sons, and his sons' sons, four generations.

And Job died, an old man, and full of days.

Context: Why do bad things happen to righteous people? The Jews were not the first to ask this question. Because they lacked a pantheon of capricious gods and goddesses to blame misfortune on, Satan is presented here as the architect of evil in the world.

Translation: Hebrew scholars point to the book of Job as the most difficult to translate in the entire Old Testament. The ancient manuscripts are conflicting, and include rare words that appear in no other surviving Hebrew texts. Translators must make educated guesses in many instances. Although it is assumed to have been written after the Babylonian exile because of the content, there is no consensus on its composition date.

Vocabulary:

Curse God: The Hebrew term, *"barak,"* meant to kneel. It is used in Job 2:9 as a euphemism, sarcastically. To "curse" God was to die, according to the Hebrews.

blessed : In Job 42:12, the Lord "blesses" Job using the same term as Job's wife: *barak* !

Meditation: Job's wife has an unfair role in this passion play. She shows up as a "bit" character to bear seven sons and three daughters...twice. Her only line is, "Curse God and die." And in the middle, Job laments that she has turned her face from him. Was Job's wife a helpmate, or not?

Job gently rebukes her. The implication seems to be that she is wondering what hidden sins are revealed by their suffering. And yet, she is also reminding him that his suffering is real.

After this interchange, his words finally begin to address his misfortunes. Job's wife forced him to deal with reality, not his idealistic hopes in Yahweh's omnipotence.

What are we to make of her silence throughout the rest of the dialogue? Women in ancient Israel were not the authors of midrash. The absence of feminine wisdom in this book would not have bothered them.

And yet, it bothers me. Do you suppose she scrounged up refreshments for him and his philosophy mates? If he truly was a righteous man, I'm sure this couple shared a few words betwixt and between soliloquies.

This isn't heaven, for sure. Job's wife was not encouraging him to denounce God, but insisted that he ditch the rose-colored glasses. We don't know all the details. But I sure would like to know what portions of his thoughts came from her.

Discussion Questions

1. Many women are thrust into the role of helping family and friends to make sense of the misfortunes of life. It requires a balance between acknowledging reality and hoping in unseen deliverance. How do we build hope?

2. Job's fortunes were restored. What does it take to develop the tenacity of Job, praising God in both times of plenty and times of want? Where are you now? Did a woman help you get there?

Chapter Eleven: Hans Urs von Balthasar and Adrienne von Speyr

Spiritual Direction for her Confessor

Near the start of World War II, Jesuit Hans Urs von Balthasar was offered a choice: teach in Rome or serve as a student chaplain in Basel (Switzerland). The Swiss native chose to return to his homeland, which was surrounded by German troops.

During the summer of 1940, he was introduced to Dr. Adrienne von Speyr, the wife of Werner Kaegi, a history professor. She was recuperating after a serious heart attack. The potential convert had been unable to pray the "Our Father" since her first husband's untimely death in 1934. Guided by Balthasar, she entered the Church months later on the Feast of All Saints. Balthasar became her spiritual director; she became the inspiration for the rest of his life's work.

Her faith and prayer crashed into his life as if it were a tsunami. He later wrote of those early years, "Immediately after her conversion, a veritable cataract of mystical graces poured over Adrienne in a seemingly chaotic storm that whirled her in all directions at once." She received graces in prayer and visions, all documented at length by Balthasar in daily dictation sessions.

It was as if she had been waiting her whole life for a confessor who could direct such an intense whirlwind. An angel visited her before Lent 1941, informing her, "Now it will begin." Every year afterward, she participated in the passion and death of Jesus Christ, including his interior sufferings, and even the stigmata.

The experiences were life altering for her and her confessor. Balthasar helped her to form the Community of St. John in 1945, composed of laywomen dedicated to the obedience and submission of St. John and the Blessed Mother standing at the foot of the cross. The group is still active today. Balthasar provided sacramental support to the group, but Adrienne von Speyr provided the spiritual direction.

In 1947, Balthasar set up a publishing house, Johannes Verlag, to publish Adrienne's works. Even so, he had trouble receiving an imprimatur for the final volumes of her commentary on the book of John. Gossip flew about Basel regarding the earnest, scholarly Jesuit who visited Frau Kaegi daily for "dictation" and meditation. Further rumors flowed from her medical practice, where certain miraculous cures were attributed to her.

About the same time, Balthasar was supposed to make his solemn religious profession in the Jesuit order. He claimed that his work with Speyr was a divine mission, and insisted that the Jesuits recognize this mission by taking on responsibility for the Community of St. John. They refused. He pushed the case all the way to the Superior General in Rome, requesting a formal investigation into the veracity of Speyr's visions, to no avail. Hans Urs von Balthasar reluctantly left the Jesuit order on February 11, 1950.

He moved to Zurich and threw himself into the tasks of writing and publishing for Johannes Verlag. To finance the books, he hit the lecture circuit. Although he was offered several professorships, he stubbornly refused. Adrienne von Speyr and her mission completely reconfigured his own assessment of his academic work. All the work of his younger years now was recast in the light of her insights.

He initially received priestly faculties from the diocesan bishop of Chur, Switzerland (Liechtenstein) and was incardinated in that diocese. In 1956, he moved in with the Kaegis, helping to care for Adrienne as her health worsened. In addition to her weak heart, she was diagnosed with both diabetes and arthritis. She was no longer able to see patients and spent her days praying, knitting and reading.

For Balthasar, the work churned on, despite his own struggles with phlebitis and later leukemia, which nearly killed him. Nevertheless, the first volume of his acclaimed Theological Aesthetics was published in 1961. The majority of his colleagues were working on the Second Vatican Council. As a "lapsed" Jesuit, he would receive no such invitation. He doggedly kept at his work on the Aesthetics, working next door to Adrienne's sickroom.

She died in 1967 from cancer of the bowel. Balthasar had refrained from sharing many of the details of her passion with others. Now free from the constraint of her effacement, he published most of the books she had dictated, corroborating the depth of her contribution to his own theological work.

The members of the Community of St. John were in awe. They had had no idea of the spiritual depth of their foundress. For them, she had simply been a friend and mentor, a humble and quiet woman who suffered much from her illnesses. Her quiet, mystical influence will be felt in theological circles for generations, thanks to her friend, Hans.

Bible Study: Proverbs 8:22 - 9:6, 13-18

Wisdom Speaks to Us

22 The LORD created me at the beginning of his work, the first of his acts of old.

23 Ages ago I was set up, at the first, before the beginning of the earth.

24 When there were no depths I was brought forth, when there were no springs abounding with water.

25 Before the mountains had been shaped, before the hills, I was brought forth;

26 before he had made the earth with its fields, or the first of the dust of the world.

27 When he established the heavens, I was there, when he drew a circle on the face of the deep,

28 when he made firm the skies above, when he established the fountains of the deep,

29 when he assigned to the sea its limit, so that the waters might not transgress his command, when he marked out the foundations of the earth,

30 then I was beside him, like a master workman; and I was daily his delight, rejoicing before him always,

31 rejoicing in his inhabited world and delighting in the sons of men.

32 And now, my sons, listen to me: happy are those who keep my ways.

33 Hear instruction and be wise, and do not neglect it.

34 Happy is the man who listens to me, watching daily at my gates, waiting beside my doors.

35 For he who finds me finds life and obtains favor from the LORD;

36 but he who misses me injures himself; all who hate me love death."

9 1 Wisdom has built her house, she has set up her seven pillars.

2 She has slaughtered her beasts, she has mixed her wine, she has also set her table.

3 She has sent out her maids to call from the highest places in the town,

4 "Whoever is simple, let him turn in here!" To him who is without sense she says,

5 "Come, eat of my bread and drink of the wine I have mixed.

6 Leave simpleness, and live, and walk in the way of insight."

13 A foolish woman is noisy; she is wanton and knows no shame.

14 She sits at the door of her house, she takes a seat on the high places of the town,

15 calling to those who pass by, who are going straight on their way,

16 "Whoever is simple, let him turn in here!" And to him who is without sense she says,

17 "Stolen water is sweet, and bread eaten in secret is pleasant."

18 But he does not know that the dead are there, that her guests are in the depths of Sheol.

Context: Wisdom "speaks" to us in these passages, as God. The style of Wisdom's instructions is similar to some Egyptian sayings attributed to the Egyptian god "Ma'at" (justice or order). However, the content is unique to the Israelites, who had no confusion about the injustice and disorder of pagan rites involving temple prostitutes and the feasts that accompanied their "sacred" rites.

Translation: The references to kings probably indicate that the Israelite royal line was still active, no later than 500 B.C. There is some evidence that this passage and the last chapter (with the famous Proverbs 31 woman) were dated earlier than the rest of the wise sayings of the book. Perhaps that explains why some of the proverbial wisdom seems to contradict itself.

Vocabulary:

master workman also could be rendered as "little child"

Wisdom: The word in Hebrew, *hokmah*, does connote a woman. *Sophia* in the Greek is also feminine.

high places: The temples in ancient times were usually placed in the highest places of a town, referring here to divine dwellings.

stolen waters: The word for water is deeply contextual. It can mean water, juice, urine, even semen. In this context, it seems to be compared to the mixed wine of Wisdom, and clearly connotes forbidden fruit.

Meditation: Being simple is a double-edged sword, then as now. Sometimes, it can mean being single-minded on just one thing. Ahem! Or it can mean being foolish. Or, it can mean not being too haughty to accept teaching. The tandem voices of Wisdom and the "foolish" women beckon the simple.

Work is required to produce food, and back then, the equation was pretty stark. The hard work involved in tilling the land and raising beasts precluded much leisure, even in secret. Even if you were wealthy enough to have slaves, you had to manage them. Illicit tomfoolery in ancient times carried with it steep consequences. One might dream of "stolen" goodies, but in fact, the upright earned their own keep.

Wisdom here is juxtaposed with sensuality. Mixed wine had water in it, served to those who were not strangers to sweat and toil. The temples of the pagans had a message that didn't recognize reality.

In our day, the exhaustion at dusk is just as likely to be mental as physical. Sedentary jobs in fluorescent cubicles are often followed by dinners in styrofoam from the drive-thru. The work of producing and consuming daily needs is almost passive. We don't even notice our physical neediness. Simplicity and insight are indeed related to one another.

The stolen water does look sweet. Yet, Wisdom's table demonstrates the loyalty of the little child. Wisdom works hard to provide the fruit of her bountiful table, and delights in that very work. Ain't no such thing as a free lunch.

Discussion Questions

1. What type of simple person are you setting your table for? Why? What's on the menu?

2. Wisdom and prudence are different but related virtues. Is there a difference? Should there be? Which is more important to you as a woman?

3. There are not many stories of an academic setting aside his whole life for a female prodigy. Hans Urs von Balthasar literally threw away his entire career. And yet, he is one of the most widely cited theologians of the 20th century today.

Chapter Twelve: Saints Mother Teresa and Pope John Paul II

A Shared Passion

They are *our* saints, the ones older Catholics who remember their lives just *knew* would be canonized. Though they never directly worked together, each recognized in the other a simpatico soul. Early on, Mother Teresa made a solemn, Albanian vow (*besos*) never to refuse Jesus anything. Pope John Paul II's motto as a bishop and then as pope was a dedication to the Blessed Virgin: "*totus tuus*," everything for you.

The entire world was their parish. They originally met in Rome, after he was already an archbishop and she had founded dozens of houses overseas for the Missionaries of Charity. Both were notable for their energy. The late pope's secretary recalled that she visited him whenever she was in town. Mother Teresa's sisters recalled her joyful countenance whenever she mentioned him.

Their early years were schools of grief and wartime privations. Mother Teresa's father died when she was only 9, possibly the victim of a political poisoning in her Balkan hometown of Skopje. She was the youngest of the three siblings, and her mother struggled to raise them. She left for the Loreto novitiate at 18.

After notable service as a Loreto sister in Calcutta, she experienced her "call within a call." After convincing her superiors of the veracity of her call, the Missionaries of Charity began with one quiet, smiling nun, sitting in the dirt with the poorest of the poor. Soon, she attracted vocations among her Indian sisters. Today, the order counts over 5000 nuns and hundreds of houses.

Pope John Paul II lived the cross as well. He was seven years old when his mother died, 14 when his brother died and a college student when the Nazis took control of Poland. After his father's death, he entered the clandestine seminary in 1942, was ordained in 1946 and earned his first doctorate in 1948.

His years in Krakow and then in academic circles in Lublin brought him to the attention of many in the hierarchy. The communists assessed his literary and academic work as cultural mishmash, and suggested his name for bishop of Krakow. He was the youngest bishop to participate in the Second Vatican Council.

Both insisted on the infinite dignity of every human being. After Mother Teresa won the Nobel Peace Prize in 1979, Pope John Paul II asked her to be his apostle of life to the nations. She humbly offered to try, demurring that it was a big job. Her big soul was up to the task; she succeeded in bringing the pro-life message to millions.

They were apostles of hope in a world too jaded to believe. What the pope had found in his compatriots despite war and brutal oppression, Mother Teresa found in the most "distressing disguise of Jesus within the poorest of the poor." In each case, they firmly held to their deep faith in the face of the suffering of millions, without once seeming to downplay the reality of that human pain. Without fear, they inspired others to believe in the possibility of God's redemption.

Billions of people were touched in some way, worldwide, by their ministries. Through television, airplane travel and modern media coverage, both were lightning rods of public acclaim. Their humility also distinguished them. Mother Teresa called herself, a "little pencil in the hand of God." To his Polish flock in Krakow, the pope retained his nickname, "Wujek." (Polish for uncle)

The recent book on Mother Teresa, *Come Be My Light*, revealed her deep interior suffering and darkness behind her constant smiles. "Faith is the substance of things hoped for, the confident assurance of things not seen." (Hebrews 11:1) Both the downfall of Eastern Bloc communism and the renewal of the Church after Vatican II are traced to John Paul the Great's pontificate.

Faith is a powerful force! Because they believed, we can have the courage to believe in what seems impossible, and to be lights of love in a dark world.

Bible Study: John 19:28-35

"I Thirst"

28 After this Jesus, knowing that all was now finished, said (to fulfil the scripture), "I thirst."

29 A bowl full of vinegar stood there; so they put a sponge full of the vinegar on hyssop and held it to his mouth. 30 When Jesus had received the vinegar, he said, "It is finished"; and he bowed his head and gave up his spirit.

31 Since it was the day of Preparation, in order to prevent the bodies from remaining on the cross on the sabbath (for that sabbath was a high day), the Jews asked Pilate that their legs might be broken, and that they might be taken away. 32 So the soldiers came and broke the legs of the first, and of the other who had been crucified with him; 33 but when they came to Jesus and saw that he was already dead, they did not break his legs. 34 But one of the soldiers pierced his side with a spear, and at once there came out blood and water. 35 He who saw it has borne witness—his testimony is true, and he knows that he tells the truth—that you also may believe.

Context: Crucifixion was introduced to the Holy Land by Greeks and Romans, though it originated likely in Phoenicia as a means of culling rebellion among slaves. Thus, it is ironic that the Son of God who came to set us free was crucified. Note also that the Romans were amenable to Jewish requests related to Sabbath prohibitions on work and arranging for burial.

Translation: The scripture that Jesus fulfilled in saying, "I thirst" was Psalm 69:21, "They gave me poison for food and for my thirst they gave me vinegar to drink." This section of the book of John also references several other Old Testament scriptures: Deut 21:23 and Ex. 12:16.

Vocabulary:

thirst: Greek: *dipsao* – the state of being thirsty Although the Greek reflects the physical thirst, the spiritual longing for the redemption of the world is seen in this passage by Mother Teresa.

vinegar: Greek *oxos*, meaning sour wine. In other gospels, it is mingled with gall. It was a common element to the crucifixions that the condemned prisoner would be given such as a kind of sedative.

hyssop: an aromatic herb used in Hebrew purification rites, which also has medicinal uses. Scholars have argued about whether its 40-50 cm length stem was long enough to truly have reached to Jesus' lips on the cross. Perhaps a reed was also used?

Meditation

(from *Come Be My Light*, pp. 260-261)

"My heart hath expected reproach and misery. And I looked for one for would grieve together with me, and there was none: and sought one that would console me, and I found none," reads the Offertory verse (Psalm 68:21) used for the Mass of the Feast of the Sacred Heart and Votive Masses of the Sacred Heart outside Easter Time. This verse triggered in Mother Teresa's memory her crucial encounter with Jesus on the train and was a permanent challenge for her to "be the one."

Years later, on a holy card of *Ecce Homo* with the printed words, "I looked for one that would comfort me and I found none," she would write, "Be the one." She loved to look at this image, a reminder of her call, and to give copies to her followers as an incentive to carry it on. She used to exhort her sisters:

Tell Jesus, "I will be the one." I will comfort, encourage and love Him....Be with Jesus. He prayed and prayed, and then we sent to look for consolation, but there was none....I always write that sentence, "I looked for one to comfort Me, but I found no one." Then I write, "Be the one." So now you be that one. Try to be the one to share with Him, to comfort Him, to console Him. So, let us ask Our Lady to help us understand.

One of the sisters remembered Mother Teresa's explanation:

"Be the one...be the one who will satiate the Thirst. Instead of saying, "I Thirst," say, "be the one"...do whatever you believe God is asking you to do to be the one to satiate Him.

Appendix: Some Thoughts on Bible Studies

"Prayer should accompany the reading of Sacred Scripture, so that a dialogue takes place between God and man. For 'we speak to him when we pray; we listen to him when we read the divine oracles." (Catechism of the Catholic Church, 2653)

There is a tension between the spiritual and intellectual approach to reading the Bible that deserves a brief note. Over the past 200 years, both Christians and even non-Christians have engaged with the Sacred Scriptures using the "historical-critical method." They have many types of analysis exploring the oral tradition behind the Old Testament as well as the handwritten copies made over the centuries. The various translations of the scriptures from the original Hebrew and Greek into modern languages also have been explored. This is called "exegesis."

It is not against Catholic doctrine to do "exegesis." The Second Vatican Council document on Scripture, The Word of God, *Dei Verbum,* states:

> *"To search out the intention of the sacred writers, attention should be given, among other things, to "literary forms." For truth is set forth and expressed differently in texts which are variously historical, prophetic, poetic, or of other forms of discourse. The interpreter must investigate what meaning the sacred writer intended to express and actually expressed in particular circumstances by using contemporary literary forms in accordance with the situation of his own time and culture. For the correct understanding of what the sacred author wanted to assert, due attention must be paid to the customary and*

characteristic styles of feeling, speaking and narrating which prevailed at the time of the sacred writer, and to the patterns men normally employed at that period in their everyday dealings with one another." (Dei Verbum 12)

At the same time, we acknowledge that exegesis by some scholars has actively sought to deter Christians from faith, and to present false teachings. Faithful Christians have rightly questioned the use of exegesis, when it leads to doubt and disunity.

The skepticism of some scholars about the One, Holy, Catholic and Apostolic Faith should not stop us from learning as much as we can to understand Sacred Scripture. We are not spiritual orphans – we have a Church dedicated to the truth. The primary point of reading the Bible, for us as Christians, is to know, love and serve God. Thus, the main purpose of Bible study is to deepen our faith.

The Bible studies found in *My Secret is Mine* Newsletter begin with some notes on the context, translation and vocabulary of the scripture passage, and the meditation is deliberately brief and leads to questions. Our sole aim is to provide interesting and relevant information that we hope will spark creative and inspiring discussions in a group setting. We sincerely seek to love Jesus more, each and every day.

The team at *My Secret is Mine* encourages you to put Jesus first. To the extent that our Bible studies are helpful, you will know them by their fruits (Matthew 7:16). And to the extent that knowing the "exegetical" details only obscures God's love for you, we encourage you and your study group to simply focus on the Word of God.

"All scripture, inspired of God, is profitable to teach, to reprove, to correct, to instruct in justice, that the man of God may be perfect, furnished to every good work." (2 Tim. 3:16-17)

A Prayer Before Reading Scripture

Spirit of wisdom, enlighten us to read your Word with the intention of both love and understanding, that we might do God's will. Help us to remember the Word as an inspiration to charity and justice. Unite our hearts with Your heart, that we might attain greater union with You. And, with Your grace, may our study benefit the souls of others with whom we share what You wish us to learn. Amen.

(based on a similar prayer by Fr. John Hardon, S.J.)

About the Author

Kristen West McGuire is the founder of Secretum Meum Mihi Press. A graduate of Georgetown University and Wesley Theological Seminary, she lives in the Lowcountry of South Carolina with her husband, a retired Marine. They have eight adult children and three wonderful grandchildren.

Read more at www.kristenwestmcguire.com.

About the Publisher

Secretum Meum Mihi Press publishes of spirituality resources content (books, newsletters, podcasts and website) for Catholic women. *Secretum Meum Mihi* is Latin for "My secret is mine," which was St. Edith Stein's response when questioned about her conversion to the Catholic faith in 1922. The flagship newsletter (www.MySecretisMine.com) includes interviews, book reviews, bible studies, prayer intentions, historical sketches and themed essays in a series. Books are based on the newsletter and suitable for parish adult study groups.

Read more at https://www.secretummeummihipress.com.

www.ingramcontent.com/pod-product-compliance
Lightning Source LLC
Chambersburg PA
CBHW030156070426
42447CB00031B/743